Families Living with Mental and Physical Challenges

THE CHANGING FACE OF MODERN FAMILIES

Families Living with Mental and Physical Challenges

Julianna Fields

Mason Crest Publishers, Inc.

MASON CREST PUBLISHERS INC.
370 Reed Road
Broomall, Pennsylvania 19008
(866)MCP-BOOK (toll free)
www.masoncrest.com

First Printing

9 8 7 6 5 4 3 2 1

ISBN 978-1-4222-1501-2
ISBN 978-1-4222-1490-9 (series)
Library of Congress Cataloging-in-Publication Data
Fields, Julianna.

Produced by Harding House Publishing Service, Inc. www.hardinghousepages.com
Interior Design by MK Bassett-Harvey.
Cover design by Asya Blue www.asyablue.com.
Printed in The United States of America.

Although the families whose stories are told in this book are made up of real people, in some cases their names have been changed to protect their privacy.

Photo Credits

Conger, Brenda 34; Creative Commons Attribution 2.0 Generic:annikaleigh 53, cupcakes2 13, organic haus 47, pedrosimoes 23; istockphoto.com 10, 13, Diloute 38, izusek 17

ontents

Introduction

The Gallup Poll has become synonymous with accurate statistics on what people really think, how they live, and what they do. Founded in 1935 by statistician Dr. George Gallup, the Gallup Organization continues to provide the world with unbiased research on who we really are.

From recent Gallup Polls, we can learn a great deal about the modern family. For example, a June 2007 Gallup Poll reported that Americans, on average, believe the ideal number of children for a family to have these days is 2.5. This includes 56 percent of Americans who think it is best to have a small family of one, two, or no children, and 34 percent who think it is ideal to have a larger family of three or more children; nine percent have no opinion. Another recent Gallup Poll found that when Americans were asked, "Do you think homosexual couples should or should not have the legal right to adopt a child," 49 percent of Americans said they should, and 48 percent said they shouldn't; 43 percent supported the legalization of gay marriage, while 57 percent did not. Yet another poll found that 34 percent of Americans feel a conflict between the demands of their professional life and their family life; 39 percent still believe that one parent should ideally stay home with the children while the other works.

Keep in mind that Gallup Polls do not tell us what is right or wrong. They don't report on what people should think—only on what they do think. And what is clear from Gallup Polls is that while the shape of families is changing in our modern world, the concept of family is still vital to our sense of who we are and how we interact with others. An indication of this is the 2008 Gallup poll that found that three out of four Americans reported that family values are important, while one in three said they are "extremely" important.

And how do Americans define "family values"? According to the same poll, here's what Americans say is their definition of a family: a strong unit where faith and morals, education and integrity play important roles within the structure of a committed relationship.

The books in the series demonstrate that strong family units come in all shapes and sizes. Those differences, however, do not change the faith, integrity, and commitment of the families who tell their stories within these books.

1 How Does Disability Change a Family?

Terms to Understand

perceive: to recognize or understand.

dysfunction: a condition where something does not work, or function, as intended.

insensitively: without consideration of the feelings or circumstances of others.

resilience: the ability to recover from illnesses or other difficulties and to continue to function well.

paraplegic: a person who is paralyzed from the waist down.

adaptation: the ability to change to deal with different circumstances or conditions.

stamina: the physical, mental, or emotional strength to endure and withstand fatigue or hardship.

mortality: death; the condition of being a human who will one day die.

autonomy: independence, freedom.

When a child can't move or *perceive* the world or think like everyone else does, we sometimes say that child has a disability. But disability does not just happen to an individual person; it happens to an entire family. Mothers, fathers, brothers, and sisters are all affected. The nature of their family will be different forever, because unlike a serious illness, disability does not get better and go away. It will always be a part of the family's reality.

This doesn't necessarily mean that these families will be worse in some way. In fact, in many ways, a disability in a family can make that family stronger. Each member of the family can learn important lessons. But a disability in the family also offers special challenges to each family member.

The individual with a disability affects both the family as a whole as well as each family member—but on the other hand, the family as whole, as well as its individual members will affect how well the person with the disability meets his or her challenges. The impact of the disability on the family and the family's response to the disability create a never-ending cycle, one that either leads to increased individual and family strength or to individual and family *dysfunction*.

As a child grows up with a disability, his family is the largest influence shaping how well he copes with his challenges. Meanwhile, his condition will put extra demands on the family. These demands include the cost involved with his medical care, special educational needs, and daily life (including what he can eat, adaptations to the family's home, and the help he needs with dressing, eating, and toileting).

All this takes time and effort, as well as money. No matter how well-intentioned and loving the family members may be, the day-to-day stress can be physically and emotionally exhausting. Worry, resentment, guilt, fear, embarrassment, and sadness are all normal reactions for family members to experience.

Each family member will have to make adjustments. Parents may have to give up or change their career goals. Marriage partners may not have as much time to devote to each other. Siblings may feel neglected or left out. Family vacations may no longer be possible. The family

According to some researchers, a disability can be defined as the gap between a person's capabilities and what the world around her expects her to be able to do in terms of personal and social roles.

home itself may need to be changed to adapt to the needs of the person with a disability. The family's relationship with the extended family and with friends may change as well. Some people outside the family may not understand the disability and react negatively and *insensitively*.

But despite these stresses and challenges, researchers have found that most adults and children who have a family member with a disability do not have psychological or emotional problems. Instead, they have found ways to cope with this added stress in their lives. Many families in this situation actually say that the disability has strength-

Families can grow closer as a unit and stronger as individuals when a member of the family has a mental or physical challenge.

ened them as a family: they have become closer; they're more accepting of others; they have a deeper faith; they've forged new friendships; they've developed a greater respect for life; and they've gained a greater confidence in their own ability to overcome challenges. Researchers refer to these characteristics as "family *resilience.*"

The families who have shared their stories in this book have all demonstrated their resilience. They have faced challenges that are not easy—but they have had the courage and the love to allow those challenges to make them stronger.

Disabilities have become a major issue for an increasing number of people. According to the World Health Organisation, 750 million people in the world have a disability. What's more, disabilities are becoming more common, mostly because modern medicine is able to keep people with disabilities alive longer.

HEADLINES

(Adapted from *Marriage and Family Encyclopedia*, family.jrank.org/pages/399/Disabilities.html)

How old a person is when a disability occurs changes the effect of that disability on both the individual and the family. When the condition is present from birth, for example, the child's entire life and identity are shaped around the disability. In some ways it may be easier for a child and his or her family to adjust to never having certain abilities than to a sudden loss of abilities later. For example, a child who was never able to walk will adapt differently than a child who suddenly becomes a *paraplegic* in adolescence due to an injury.

A disability can be one of three things:

- a physical impairment (the inability to move like other people do)
- a sensory impairment (the inability to perceive the world the way other people do, such as blindness or deafness)
- an intellectual impairment (the inability to think and process the world mentally the way other people do)

The age of the parents when a child's disability is diagnosed is also an important consideration in how the family responds. For example, teenage parents are at greater risk for experiencing poor *adaptation* because their own developmental needs are still prominent, and they are less likely to have the maturity and resources to cope with the added demands of the child. Older parents meanwhile may lack the *stamina* for the extra burden of care required, and they may fear their own *mortality* and be concerned about who will care for their child when they die.

Developmental tasks of adolescence— developing an identity and developing greater *autonomy*—are particularly difficult when the adolescent has a disability. Part of this process for most adolescents generally involves some risk-taking behaviors, such as smoking and drinking. Adolescents with disabilities take risks too, sometimes defying treatment and procedures related to their condition, such as skipping medications or changing a prescribed diet. Issues related to sexuality may be particularly difficult because the person with disability has fears about his or her desirability to a partner, sexual performance, and worries about ever getting married or having children. . . .

The initial response of most families to the sudden onset of disability is to pull together and rally around the person affected and provide support to each other. Some or all family members may suspend their daily routines for a period of time as they focus on the immediate crisis. They gather more information about the condition, its course, treatment options, and where to get services. Often there are new behaviors to be learned, including how to provide care and treatment to the person with the disability, how to interact with health care and other service providers, and how to access needed information. There is also a whole set of emotional issues that confronts family members, including grief over the loss of abili-

Both parents and siblings learn to help care for the family member with a disability. This ability to work together and to overcome obstacles gives confidence and strength to the entire family.

ties; worry about the future and the costs; feelings of guilt, blame, or responsibility; and trying to find a cause and a meaning for this event. Families are more variable in how they deal with these emotional challenges. Some avoid them altogether and stay focused on gathering information and learning new behaviors. Other families are split, with some members having intense emotional reactions and others avoiding them. Even though there is the expectation that family members should provide support to each other in times of crisis, this is often unrealistic when members are out of sync with each other and each person needs so much. Families often need help to get through this stage, and it is vitally important that they receive it. In many ways their early response sets the stage for how the family will adapt to the disability over the long run.

Following this *crisis* phase, there is the *chronic* phase of living with a disability. This phase varies in length depending on the condition, but it is essentially the "long haul," when the family settles into living with the disability. The ultimate challenge to the family is to meet the disability-related needs and simultaneously to meet the needs of the family and its members of having a normal life. A metaphor used to describe this challenge is "finding a place for the disability in the family, but keeping the disability in its place."

> The parents in families where a child has a disability are more apt to experience stress and tension in their relationship—but research shows that these families are no more apt to go through a divorce than any other family.

What Do You Think?

Why do you think it is particularly hard to be an adolescent with a disability? What do you think the author means when he says that families need to "find a place for the disability in the family but keep the disability in its place"?

2 Families Living with Mental Illness

Terms to Understand

social workers: professionals trained to help people deal with difficulties caused by illnesses, disabilities, or poverty, often by helping them work through the systems already in place to provide assistance.

chronic: continuing for a long period of time.

hallucinations: sensory experiences existing only in the mind, seeming real to the individual experiencing them.

delusions: false beliefs or opinions, held strongly in spite of all evidence.

flat affect: severely reduced emotional expressiveness.

cognitive deficits: any characteristic keeping a person from experiencing the full range of intellectual abilities, whether affecting all areas of thought or only certain aspects.

psychosocial factors: anything having to do with a person's mental condition, finances, or relationships with other people that contributes to a specific result.

Aaron Booker was one of those kids who seemed to have it all.

His parents, Bernie and Nancy, seldom worried about him or his brother David. From middle school on, Aaron's good looks and smooth manners had made him popular with the ladies. He flew through high school, getting A's in every subject and a letter in wrestling on his varsity jacket. College was a breeze, too. He entered it with scholarships and emerged from it with a master's degree in accounting.

Job hunting, for Aaron, meant a single interview at IBM, which then offered him a middle-management position. "He was really up there in income, right off the bat," Nancy says. Within a year he was promoted and given a healthy raise. It looked like Aaron's future knew no bounds.

And then, at age 29, he started hearing voices.

Bernie and Nancy would hear him murmuring to himself in the kitchen sometimes when he visited them. They didn't think much of it, until one day Nancy paused outside the door and listened more closely. It was as if Aaron was on the phone, answering somebody's ques-

Individuals with schizophrenia sometimes hear and respond to voices that others cannot hear. Often, they fear that other people are plotting against them.

tions—but he wasn't. With a chill, she realized he was responding to a voice no one else could hear.

"He seemed uncoordinated, too," she said. "He'd fall down stairs, like he was unbalanced. And he had this really bad cough."

But he didn't smoke—not legal or illegal substances—take drugs, or drink. So what was going on? No one in either her or Bernie's family had ever been mentally ill. What was suddenly happening to their son?

Aaron, who had an apartment nearby, had made it a habit to visit his parents daily at suppertime, so he could indulge in his mother's good cooking. Now they watched him intently, realizing he was changing day by day.

He looked at Nancy with suspicion, saying the food tasted different—and then he'd throw it away.

His speech patterns were different—he seemed to be talking faster and less logically than usual—which seemed to reflect his scattered thoughts.

"He got a flat, pale look on his face, too," Nancy says.

And it seemed his suspiciousness grew with each day. He said he was worried that other people in his department at work wanted him to be fired; that people on the street were out to get him, although he didn't know why. When he talked like that he seemed to be terrified, but nothing his parents or brother could say allayed his fears.

Schizophrenia is a *chronic*, severe, and disabling brain disorder that in a given year affects about 1.1 percent of the U.S. population ages 18 and older. People with schizophrenia sometimes hear voices others don't hear; they may believe that others are broadcasting their thoughts to the world, or become convinced that others are plotting to harm them. These experiences can make them fearful and withdrawn and cause difficulties when they try to have relationships with others.

He was having more and more trouble sleeping—Nancy and Bernie knew that because they'd hear their TV on at all hours of the night, after Aaron had apparently let himself into their living room.

He'd be gone in the morning, though, in plenty of time to get ready for work. And he maintained his appearance and kept his apartment neat and clean. In some respects, he functioned normally. In other ways, though, he was a wreck.

Mental Health Arrests

Under the mental-hygiene law, police officers can arrest someone if they suspect he may harm himself or someone else as a result of mental-health problems. Usually, the person will be taken to a psychiatric emergency care program, a facility that will be staffed with psychiatrists, psychiatric nurses, and *social workers*. Patients have to be evaluated by a staff psychiatrist within 48 hours of admittance, and they can be held involuntarily up to 72 hours (or longer if specific standards are met.) Mental-hygiene arrests of young people, children, and adolescents are often made in schools, where principals are typically the ones who make the emergency call to police when children's behavior can't be managed in a classroom setting.

Aaron was an adult now and his parents couldn't bully him into getting help, so they tried to gently persuade him to tell his doctor what was happening. Nothing worked. Then one day, Nancy came home and found that Aaron had barricaded himself in their bathroom. Behind the door, he was screaming. The words made no sense to her, but she was terrified. She called Bernie, she called David—and finally they called the police.

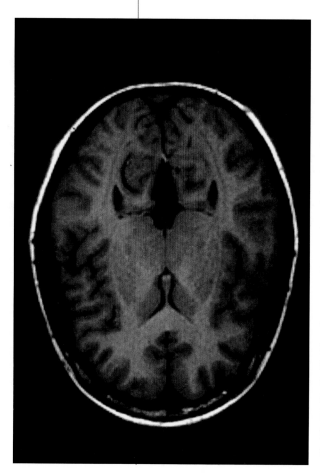

The police talked to Aaron through the bathroom door, but their voices only seemed to upset him more. Nancy could hear him sobbing, and she felt as though her heart would break. The police refused to take him away, though. It still had to be Aaron's choice to get help.

That changed when Aaron started talking about killing

There is no lab test for schizophrenia—a psychiatrist usually makes the diagnosis based on clinical observation of symptoms. Brain imaging, like the MRI shown here, is being tested as a possible physical diagnostic test.

himself. This time when Bernie called the police, they took him away to a psychiatric hospital.

"We had to have the police do it," she says. "There was no way we could do it. He was too old, too big."

Aaron was hospitalized for 72 hours, but he had quickly calmed down once the police took him away. A psychiatrist had examined him, but decided to release him. Nancy was both relieved—and frightened. By now, she was sure Aaron had a serious problem that needed medical attention.

Just the Facts

Schizophrenia's symptoms usually develop in men in their late teens or early twenties and women in their twenties and thirties, but in rare cases, they can appear in childhood. Symptoms can include *hallucinations*, *delusions*, disordered thinking, movement disorders, *flat affect*, social withdrawal, and *cognitive deficits*. People with schizophrenia may not make sense when they talk, they may sit for hours without moving or talking much, or they may seem perfectly fine until they talk about what they are really thinking. Because many people with schizophrenia have difficulty holding a job or caring for themselves, their condition places a heavy burden on their families and on society.

Finally, Aaron's behavior at work fell apart as well. This time his boss at work was the one who called the police. Aaron was once again hospitalized—and this time he was diagnosed with schizophrenia.

Two years before, Aaron had been every parent's perfect son, every company's ideal employee. Now, on a leave of absence from the job of his dreams, he was diagnosed with a serious and incurable mental illness.

The more Bernie and Nancy read about schizophrenia, the more they found to fear. Medication can largely control the symptoms—but once the medication is effective, the person may come to believe he no longer needs to take it. Each anti-psychotic medicine has some sort of objectionable side effect, such as constipation or diarrhea, Parkinson-like tremors or shuffling, and weight gain. Some of those reactions are so annoying the patient may begin to think he's better off without the medication.

And because the disease affects the mind, the person may not realize just how much he needs the medication. When overwhelmed by symptoms, he may not be able to look at his situation rationally and or recognize the way to correct it.

It took months, but doctors found the ideal blend of prescriptions to let Aaron lead a reasonably normal life. He tried to go back to work, but found he could no longer do the job. His professional life was over, and he had no choice but to accept that his life would never be the same. His disease could be managed—but it would require his full attention to do it.

Aaron is 52 now. Bernie, Nancy, and David have built their family life around Aaron's needs, and thanks to their support and effort, he has never been homeless, a fate that sometimes befalls those with mental illness. He drives a good car, pays his bills on time, and keeps his room neat. On the street, he looks like anyone else. He keeps his hair trimmed and clothes tidy. Generally, his medications are so effective that no one would guess he's schizophrenic.

An estimated 20–25% of the nearly 700,000 homeless Americans suffer from some form of mental illness.

HEADLINES

(Adapted from: www.schizophrenia.com/family/FAQsibs. htm#sibeffect)

If your brother or sister has schizophrenia, all of the following feelings are absolutely normal. Don't be afraid to share your feelings with someone you trust—and don't think it means you have a psychiatric disorder too if you may need to talk to a counselor to get help dealing with your feelings.

• Confusion about the way your sibling acts
• Embarrassment or shame about being in your sibling's company, or having to explain their illness to your friends
• Jealousy of parent's attention to your ill brother or sister
• Anger that such a bad thing could happen to a person like your brother/sister.
• Frustration at your parents, doctors, or the mental health care system if you don't feel included in recovery/treatment plans.
• Resentment at not having a "normal" family, and having to deal with this burden for the rest of your life
• Grief over the loss of a sibling that you knew and loved, and the loss of a normal childhood
• Pressure to be the "perfect son or daughter," to not cause any trouble and succeed at everything

• Fear: of maybe becoming sick yourself, of eventually having to care for your ill sibling, or of a child of your own someday who ends up with schizophrenia.

But his illness leaves its mark on the family in quiet ways, even when he's at his best. "Many of our extended family won't invite him to holiday gatherings," Nancy says, "They're afraid, although they don't need to be. It means that our family—the four of us—are separated from the rest of the larger family. It makes me sad—but it also makes me angry. My son never asked to be ill."

It takes courage being a part of a family where one member has mental illness. "We're always waiting for the other shoe to drop," Nancy says, "for the next crisis to hit." Nancy describes these times—when Aaron suddenly goes off balance for no apparent reason—as "pure hell."

"One time he wouldn't get out of his car and the police had to smash the window. He thought they were trying to get him—they were, so they could take him to the crisis center," Nancy says.

Nancy and Bernie grieve that their handsome, intelligent son missed so much because of his illness. "Life passed him by," Nancy says. "He couldn't have a family or a wife."

Aaron hasn't had a major episode for a year and a half—and that's a record for him, according to Nancy. Maybe he'll stay well now; she and Bernie really hope so, because they're both getting older, and there will

How Do Families Cope?

In her book *Troubled Journey*, author Diane T. Marsh describes the strengths and resources that allow a family to cope when a member has schizophrenia:

- strong family bonds
- family pride in your accomplishments together, and those of your loved one with schizophrenia
- continued growth, both as a family unit and as individual members, even in the face of challenges
- good mental and physical health among other family members
- adequate financial/educational resources
- a strong support system, inside and outside the family
- spiritual resources that help you make sense out of life

Factors that prevent a family from effectively coping:

- denial of the mental illness by family members
- disruption and stress from other circumstances
- unhealthy coping strategies (such as substance abuse)
- family disintegration such as divorce

come a time when they will no longer be able to look out for Aaron. They know that David is also committed to his brother, but he has married now, and has his own life to live.

As many as 51 million people worldwide suffer from schizophrenia. In each country the prevalence is the same—about 0.5–1% of the population.

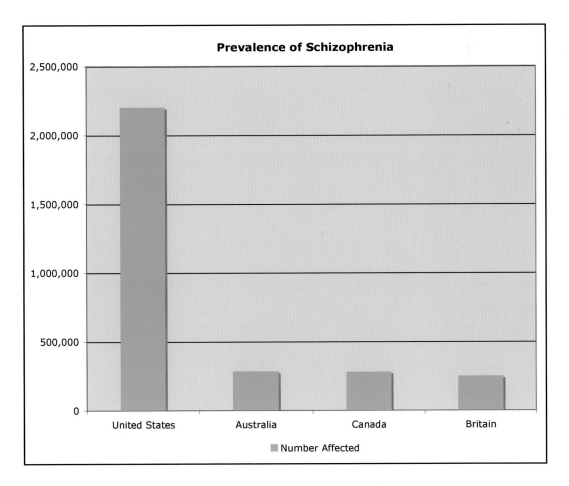

"You think your kids will grow up and then they won't need you any more," Nancy says. "But in Aaron's case, that didn't turn out to be true. Being Aaron's mother takes up more of my energy now than it did when he was younger. We've built our family around him. I've learned to not think about how scared I am, only about how much I love my son. But I don't know what the future will hold for him."

What Do You Think?

Imagine how you would feel if you were David, Aaron's brother. What decisions do you think you would make about your brother's care once your parents were too old to be responsible for him?

HEADLINES

(From the National Institute of Mental Health, www.nimh.nih.gov/health/publications/schizophrenia)

Scientists agree that schizophrenia runs in families. It occurs in 1 percent of the general population but is seen in 10 percent of people with a first-degree relative (a parent, brother, or sister) with the disorder. People who have second–degree relatives (aunts, uncles, grandparents, or cousins) with the disease also develop schizophrenia more often than the general population. The identical twin of a person with schizophrenia is most at risk, with a 40 to 65 percent chance of developing the disorder.

Our genes are located on 23 pairs of chromosomes that are found in each cell. We inherit two copies of each gene, one from each parent. Several of these genes are thought to be associated with an increased risk of schizophrenia, but scientists believe that each gene has a very small effect and is not responsible for causing the disease by itself. It is still not possible to predict who will develop the disease by looking at genetic material.

Although there is a genetic risk for schizophrenia, it is not likely that genes alone are sufficient to cause the disorder. Interactions between genes and the environment are thought to be necessary for schizophrenia to develop. Many environmental factors have been suggested as risk factors, such as exposure to viruses or malnutrition in the womb, problems during birth, and *psychosocial factors*, like stressful environmental conditions.

What Do You Think?

How does this article explain the connection between schizophrenia and families? How do you think it would affect a family where more than one member had schizophrenia?

HEADLINES

(From CNN Interactive, www.cnn.com/HEALTH/9810/15/schizo. reality/)

[Many people have] a frightening image of schizophrenia. But more often than not, that image is not accurate for many who suffer from the disorder.

Charlie Chastain said most people are surprised to find out he has schizophrenia. He developed the telltale signs of the brain disease when he was 15. . . . Chastain's parents were told to expect the worst.

"He would spend the majority of his life in a locked facility and we'd be visiting on holidays, and the family should be prepared to adjust to that," Mary Ella Chastain said.

But that's not how life turned out for Charlie Chastain. Now 27, he has a college degree in psychology and a full-time job as an advocate for mental health patients in Clayton County, Georgia. He leads a support group for the mentally ill and hopes one day to go to graduate school.

Chastain attributes much of his success to finding the right medication four years after his first break with reality. "I really think that if I went off my medicine, I would end up in a psychiatric hospital," he said.

Following a strict regimen of medication helps many schizophrenics live with their ailment. That fear motivates him to continue his treatment. Unfortunately, among people with schizophrenia, Chastain is the exception, not the rule.

What Do You Think?

When you see someone who has mental illness like Charlie Chastain or Aaron, do you think they are frightening? Why or why not? Why do you think Charlie has been so successful at handling his disease? Although this article does not say, why do you think Charlie may have been able to find the right medication when so many people with his condition are not able to?

Terms to Understand

developmental delays: occurrences of growth milestones (such as walking, talking, etc.) not being reached at the expected age.

genetic testing: tests to identify changes to chromosomes and genes, generally to confirm or rule out genetic disorders.

empathize: to feel understanding about what another person is experiencing.

advocacy: the act of arguing for or supporting a person or cause.

hereditary: being passed, or able to be passed, from parent to child through the genes.

neural tube defect: any of a number of abnormalities caused when an embryo's neural tube—the beginnings of the central nervous system—fails to close completely during development.

embryo: an organism in its early stages of development, before birth.

diversity: variety.

ambulatory: able to walk.

mobility: the ability to move freely.

neurological: relating to nerves and the nervous system.

accommodations: things providing for needs or wants.

amplify: make stronger.

competency: having the needed skills, abilities, or knowledge.

3 Families Living with Physical Challenges

Cliff and Brenda Conger are proud of their family. Their oldest daughter Paige is on the dean's list at the Fashion Institute of Technology in New York City, and her unique designs have already been seen in the Big Apple's fashion shows. She plans to be famous, her mom says. Being the talented over-achiever she has always been, Paige Conger may soon make her mark in fashion circles both national and international. Meanwhile, in a very different realm, Paige's sixteen-year-old brother Cliffy has already become famous nationwide. His face beams at visitors to the website of CFC International (www.cfcsyndrome.org), a group begun by his mom after Cliffy was diagnosed with a rare genetic disorder called Cardiofaciocutaneous (CFC) syndrome.

Cliffy is one of an estimated 200 to 300 individuals in the entire United States with the incurable condition. As its name suggests, it affects the heart ("cardio"), face ("facio"), and skin ("cutaneous") of its victims—but that's really just the start. Some symptoms are obvious: CFC patients' heads are unusually large with pronounced foreheads and sparse hair; their eyes have droopy eyelids and may not have eyelashes or brows. Their skin

CFC is the result of mutations on genes such as the BRAF gene, which provides instructions for making a protein that helps transmit chemical signals from outside the cell to the cell's nucleus. The yellow arrow shows the location of the BRAF gene on chromosome 7.

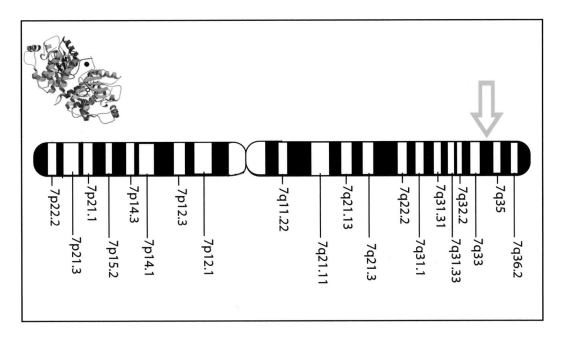

can be thickened, coarse, extremely dry or have some other abnormal texture—and CFC patients tend to be short in stature. *Developmental delays* and learning difficulties are a part of the syndrome, but they can vary dramatically from child to child.

Cliffy struggles physically because of poor muscle tone caused by his CFC. Every year he looks forward to the spring, when he gets to ride the John Deere tractor.

"Cliffy can learn better than most children with CFC," says Brenda, "but physically he struggles. His low muscle tone makes his walk more of a slow shuffle."

What can't be seen just by looking at a young person like Cliffy is the head-to-toe set of internal medical complexities that require intervention and constant monitoring, such as heart defects and digestive difficulties that can prevent the child from absorbing nutrients from food, even as a baby.

"Each hour in the Neonatal Intensive Care unit brought news from another specialist of more compiling defects," Brenda wrote on the website, describing the early days of Cliffy's life. "This was not a total shock since we had traveled out of state during the pregnancy to consult with a high risk medical team who then warned us that possible syndrome children are usually born with a cluster of defects."

Cliffy, like many newborns with CFC, couldn't regulate his breathing and swallowing. For many families, feeding tubes become just one more routine in dealing with their child.

In the course of her training and career to become a special education teacher long before she had children, Brenda had seen and worked with many types of disability. Her knowledge, combined with the emotions involved in having a child with many serious problems, contributed to an overwhelming sense of grief she couldn't shake for months.

"I had seen institutionalized people who couldn't coordinate their breathing and swallowing," she says. "I knew we were looking at a severely and profoundly disabled individual."

Her husband Cliff, owner of a ski shop, coped much better initially, she says—although Cliff remembers being "like a zombie" for the first three months. They not only had a medically complicated newborn to deal with—they had a little daughter who needed their care and attention, too.

Doctors had trouble pinning a name to Cliffy's ever-growing list of symptoms and abnormalities. It wasn't

CFC is caused by genetic mutations—changes in one of four different genes. No one knows exactly why these changes occur, but scientists know that CFC does not run in families. Currently, there is no cure to treat all the symptoms of CFC syndrome. However, with proper management and early treatment, much can be done to improve the health of children with CFC syndrome. At present, treatment ultimately depends on the unique needs of each individual. These can include heart surgery to repair a structural defect, medications and lotions for the skin problems, or eye surgeries or corrective lenses to improve vision.

until *genetic testing* had been done, that the doctors settled on a diagnosis of CFC.

By then the three-year-old boy had seen more specialists and endured more tests and treatments than most people do in a lifetime—and the torment of needles and procedures would likely be part of Cliffy's life forever.

That was the hardest part, Brenda says: Watching her son's pain and hearing his screams—but knowing they had no choice, if they wanted to give Cliffy the best quality life he could have. What the letters "CFC" really stood for, some parents claimed, was "Constantly Facing Challenges."

And the challenges weren't only medical. Many CFC kids can never speak or function anywhere near their age level. "For some families, going out in public is a big problem, because of behavioral issues and seizure disorders which are often very difficult to control," Brenda says. "We've been blessed not to have those issues with Clifford."

Many families of kids with disabilities find that one of their biggest challenges is giving equal attention to all children in the family, not just the one with the most needs.

Paige and Cliff interacted like any brother and sister, but their relationship holds an extra tenderness. Big-sister Paige has always been a part of helping Cliffy be all that he can be.

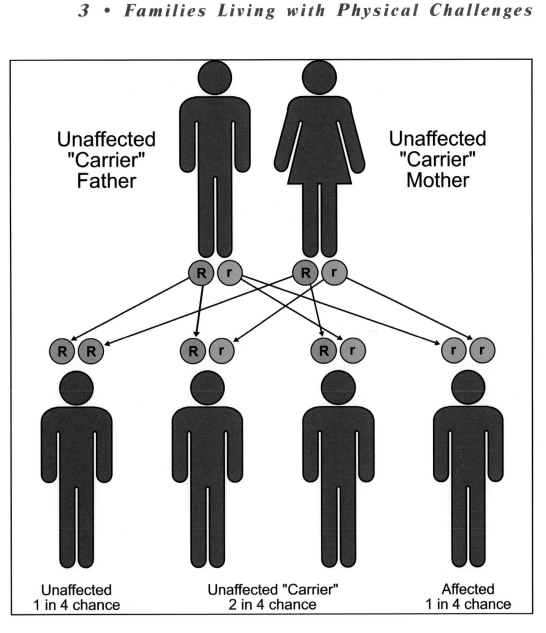

Unaffected
"Carrier"
Father

Unaffected
"Carrier"
Mother

Unaffected
1 in 4 chance

Unaffected "Carrier"
2 in 4 chance

Affected
1 in 4 chance

The random mutation that causes CFC does not run in families. Unlike CFC, Cystic fibrosis, an autosomal recessive genetic disorder, is inherited when both parents contribute genes with the mutation.

Not all CFC kids are as expressive, or as high-functioning, as Cliffy. In a series for the *Toronto Globe and Mail*, reporter Ian Brown tells the ongoing and intimate story of his own CFC child, Walker. He speaks of the exhaustion of sleepless nights, the frustration of watching Walker hit and kick himself, the knowledge that this boy will never be able to put his feelings into words.

Siblings of children with a mental or physical disability are often involved in the care of their brother or sister from a young age. This closeness can lead to a very special sibling bond.

Brown talks of a language they share: clicking. He makes a clicking sound with his mouth, and Walker clicks back. That's what passes for conversation between them, he says—but under the circumstances, it's an important exchange.

Sometimes Brenda and other CFC parents ponder the reason for the circumstances that have been dropped in their laps. She has seen many marriages stressed to the breaking point in CFC families, and some parents need to rely on in-home services

For her personally, having Cliffy has been a growth experience, Brenda says. Because of her academic background, she knew, intellectually, about special-needs children, but she couldn't truly *empathize* with their mothers and fathers until she found herself walking in their shoes. "I didn't understand how draining it is to parents," she says.

She has since moved from teaching into an *advocacy* position in the high school, where she works with parents of children with special needs. Thanks to Cliffy, now when she talks to families, she can meet the adults on their own level and help them understand how to be more effective in meeting their child's needs.

Some parents give up and walk away, she says. "We have a huge percentage of kids in our schools—including those with disabilities—who just don't have supports behind them," she says. Some of them have been turned out of their homes and live with friends or relatives.

Many physical challenges are congenital; this means they were present at birth. Congenital physical disabilities include:

- *muscular dystrophy*: a group of hereditary diseases that make the muscles become weaker and weaker.
- *cystic fibrosis*: a hereditary disease that affects the mucus glands of the lungs, liver, pancreas, and intestines. Abnormally thick mucus makes these body organs unable to work properly. Children with cystic fibrosis have frequent lung infections. Their digestive systems are unable to work correctly, which interferes with their ability to grow normally.

Other physical challenges can be caused by an accident or a disease that occurs later in a person's life. Either way, families must learn to cope together.

In creating the CFC International website, she wanted to give families touched by the syndrome a place where they could vent, learn from each other, and contribute to the general base of knowledge about this rare disorder. Ultimately what she did was create a first-of-its-kind CFC registry, which serves as an valuable resource for researchers.

Although CFC is very rare, it is one of numerous other genetic syndromes. Brenda's work and attitude is an inspiration for other parents dealing with similar circumstances.

Cliff and his son head for the John Deere tractor at the first sign of spring. Cliffy's greatest joy in life is driving it around the family's four-acre property. He can't ride a bike because of his poor muscle tone; he'll never drive a car. But he loves riding the tractor.

Cliffy may have limitations. He may not live as long as he would if CFC wasn't part of his world. But Cliff, Brenda, and Paige are proud of him—and despite the difficulties they've faced and the mountains of challenges they know still await them, they're thankful Cliffy is part of their family and their lives.

What Do You Think?

How would you feel if you had a little brother like Cliffy? What would be hard about it? What parts would you enjoy?

HEADLINES

(Adapted from "Welcoming Babies with Spina Bifida" by Judy Rowley,
June 2007, www.waisman.wisc.edu/~Rowley/sb-kids/wbwsb.html)

Spina bifida is a *neural tube defect* that occurs in one out of every 1,000 newborns in the United States. In Canada, one in every 750 babies is born with spina bifida. Spina bifida occurs within the first four weeks of pregnancy, before many women are aware that they are pregnant. For some unexplained reason, the *embryo's* neural tube (which develops into the brain, spinal cord, and vertebral column) fails to form properly, which results in varying degrees of permanent damage to the spinal column and the nervous system. . . .

One question frequently asked by parents of newborns who have spina bifida, or parents who have found out that their unborn child has spina bifida is, "How will this affect my child?" There is great *diversity* among the population of people who have spina bifida. . . .

Some children born with spina bifida will be *ambulatory*. A few will walk without assistance; others will require bracing and a walker or crutches. Some children who walk when they are younger will find that using a wheelchair for most activities makes sense as they grow so they can keep up with their friends.

Some children with spina bifida will first start using a wheelchair for *mobility* when they are a just few years old. Some children will find that a manual chair fits their needs. Other children who use a manual chair when they are quite young may find that a power wheelchair gives them more independence of mobility when they get a little older.

The important thing to remember is that regardless of the level of *neurological* involvement, people with spina bifida are more like typically developing individuals than they are different. They have a full range of emotions and attitudes, are creative and imaginative in play and pranks, and grow up to live independent lives with varying degrees of support and *accommodations* needed. . . .

Parents of children with spina bifida have concerns about how a child with spina bifida will affect their marriage or other children. Unfortunately, there are some medical practitioners who give families outdated information regarding the rate of divorce in families with a child who has disabilities. Several years ago, there were a few studies published which suggested that the rate of divorce in such families was higher than in families without a child with disabilities. However, since then, there have been multiple studies which show that families with a child with disabilities have the same rates of divorce as other

families. Many parents find that having a child with disabilities tends to *amplify* life experiences—strong marriages grow stronger, weak marriages may show more signs of strain.

Brothers and sisters of children with disabilities have concerns similar to those experienced by their parents. In addition, they face issues that are unique to siblings of children with disabilities. Fortunately, there is a growing body of research and resources to help parents ensure that siblings of children with disabilities feel informed and supported. . . .

As parents of infants and toddlers it can be difficult to envision our children as independent young adults. As parents of youngsters who have high medical and personal care needs, it can be difficult to envision a time when our children will be living on their own, making important decisions and directing their own lives. But the independent living skills our children will need 15 or 20 years from now need to have their foundations laid today. It is important to foster our child's self-esteem and *competency* by providing them ample opportunities to play an active part in their own care.

Most children with spina bifida have normal or above normal intelligence. Some children with spina bifida may experience learning difficulties. Some children with spina bifida may need special testing to help educators understand how to best to accommodate their learning needs. It is important to remember that these tests do not measure many important areas of intelligence, and you will often be surprised by the insight, creativity, wit and humor of your child. . . .

Thousands of young people with spina bifida across the country are quietly going on with their lives and transforming their communities by just being there. They have dreams and the determination to reach their goals. They learn in regular classrooms in their neighborhood schools with the children who will one day be their co-workers, neighbors and adult friends. Young adults hold diverse and meaningful jobs, maintain their own households, and make significant contributions to their communities every day.

What Do You Think?

Children with physical disabilities were once separated in school from so-called "normal" children. How do you think the author of this article would feel about that? Do you think it is good for all kinds of children to be in the same classroom? Why or why not?

4 Families Living with Intellectual Disabilities

From the earliest days of their marriage, Josephine and Joseph (their friends called them JoJo and Joe) Palumbo knew they wanted a family. JoJo's heart was waiting to embrace some special little people. She and Joe, who had a good job with the city streets crew, owned their own three-bedroom home, and Joe wanted nothing more than for his wife to be a stay-at-home mom as his own mother had been. His father, a quiet and somewhat distant man, had been the breadwinner and disciplinarian, while Joe's mother had been the one with the big heart. Joe expected those roles to carry over into his home, too.

Life did not go quite as they'd planned, however. Despite their wishes, JoJo was unable to conceive for the first eighteen years of their marriage. When she finally

did, she was forty-one. She refused her doctor's sugges-
tion for amniocentesis, a test that would determine if
her baby had any abnormalities.

"It doesn't matter," she told the doctor. "Joe and I
will love this child no matter what."

In her heart, she already had a suspicion that her
baby might not be the same as other children. As an
older mother, she knew the odds were greater that she
might have a child with a genetic anomaly like Down
syndrome. Something told her to prepare herself emotionally—and she did her research and found out everything she could about this syndrome.

These three-month-old twins are not identical; the baby
on the left has Down syndrome. Even at this young age,
the differences in facial feature development and size are
already apparent.

The day finally came—after almost twenty years of longing—and their daughter Celeste was born. One look at the doctor's face as he looked down at her newborn child, and JoJo's heart skipped a beat. Something was wrong. Her *intuition* had been right.

"There's a problem with your baby," the doctor told the Palumbos a little later. "She has Down syndrome."

Joe was silent, but JoJo struggled to sit up in bed. "Okay, but what's wrong?" she asked, trying to keep her voice calm as she struggled to control her anxiety.

"She has Down syndrome," the doctor said again.

"Yes, but what's wrong?"

"I don't think you understand," the doctor said. "She will never be able to learn like other children, and she will have—"

"So that's all that's wrong?" Tears of relief ran down JoJo's cheeks. "If Down syndrome is the only thing wrong with her, then that's no problem at all for us."

Joe nodded. He too was more than ready to accept the challenge their new daughter offered. If his wife felt she could handle a child with disabilities, it was fine by him.

As it turned out, Celeste was lucky; she did not have any of the major medical problems that were often part of the syndrome, and those she did have were managed with medications. JoJo devoted all day, every day, to helping Celeste make the most of her *potential*.

Down syndrome was named after the British doctor, John Langdon Down, who first described the condition in 1887. Doctors did not know that an extra chromosome caused the syndrome, though, until 1959.

Down syndrome, also called Trisomy 21, is a condition in which extra genetic material causes delays in the way a child develops, both mentally and physically. About 1 in every 800 babies is born with this condition.

Normally, at the time of conception a baby inherits genetic information from its parents in the form of 46 chromosomes: 23 from the mother and 23 from the father. In most cases of Down syndrome, a child gets an extra chromosome 21, for a total of 47 chromosomes instead of 46. It's this extra genetic material that causes the physical features and developmental delays associated with this syndrome.

Although no one knows for sure why DS occurs and there's no way to prevent the chromosomal error that causes it, scientists do know that women age 35 and older have a much higher risk of having a child with the condition. At age 30, for example, a woman has about a 1 in 900 chance of conceiving a child with DS. Those odds increase to about 1 in 350 by age 35. By 40 the risk rises to about 1 in 100.

Speech therapy trained Celeste's reluctant mouth to form sounds others could understand. Another therapist worked with Celeste to help her learn to use her fingers more easily. Fortunately their community was rich in resources for those with disabilities, and the

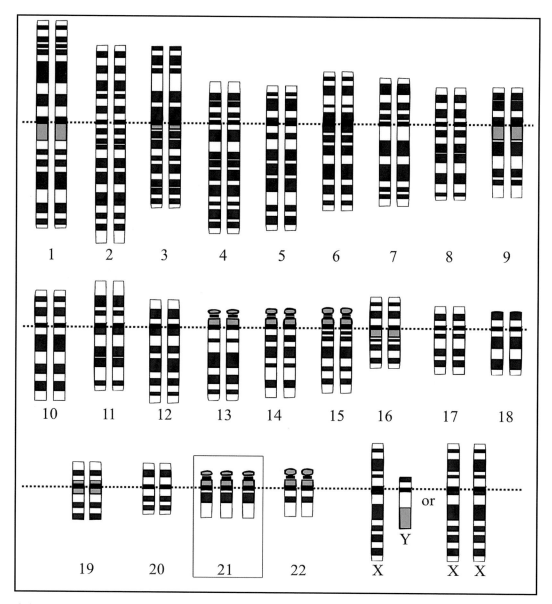

A karyotype shows the number and appearance of the chromosomes in the cell nuclei of an organism. This example shows the karyotype for Down syndrome—the third copy of chromosome 21 gives the syndrome the alternate name Trisomy 21.

Palumbos lived within easy driving distance of those facilities. Families who lived in rural areas often had a more difficult time—if the mother and father both held down jobs, transporting the child to distant therapeutic centers regularly was nearly impossible.

Meanwhile, Celeste grew older. She did not learn to walk or talk as soon as other children her age, but she could and did learn.

One day when Celeste was three years old, Joe walked in the door with something lumpy—and wiggly—inside his jacket. Celeste squealed as a tiny silken-haired puppy peeked out. "Aa-eee!" she exclaimed.

With the addition of a couple consonants, JoJo turned her daughter's exclamation of joy into a name for their golden retriever: "Hayley."

Celeste couldn't speak yet, but her eyes and expression indicated that she certainly had opinions. JoJo got books on American Sign Language out of the library and began to teach herself and Celeste simple words. Little did she know Hayley was paying attention, too.

One day Celeste made the sign for "cookie"—and with JoJo watching in amazement, Hayley stretched to reach the countertop. She closed her mouth around the box of cookies and took them to Celeste's place at the table.

Pretty soon the little girl and the young dog knew the words for "ball," "bone," "outside," and "kiss"—and used them with regularity.

Children with Down syndrome are more likely to have heart defects, gastroesophageal reflux disease, recurrent ear infections, obstructive sleep apnea, and thyroid dysfunctions.

Most children with Down syndrome have difficulty coordinating their muscles, including the muscles in their lips and tongues. This means that many children with Down syndrome do not learn to speak until they are much older than other children. In some cases, these children do have the mental ability to learn language, even though they lack the ability to shape their mouths into words. Teaching children like this sign language allows them to begin communicating earlier than they might otherwise be able to.

Fully accepted by those around her, Celeste grew into a sunny, outgoing child. When she started pre-kindergarten she made a flock of little friends. She was smaller than all of them, and one girl in her class insisted on carrying Celeste around as if she were a doll. At story time and nap time, children jockeyed for a position near her. Celeste, her teacher said, was one of the most popular kids in the class—never mind that she was the only one with a disability.

JoJo was a familiar face in the classroom. "That woman was made to be the mother of that child," noted Lavinia Armstrong, one of Celeste's teachers. "The love and care she gives Celeste is one of the reasons that little girl does so well academically and socially."

That degree of attention came at a cost, though JoJo never complained. By nature, however, she wasn't a patient person. She would admit that having to show Celeste how to brush her teeth over and over and over again taxed her sometimes.

Meanwhile, Joe had his own adjustment issues. Both husband and wife had come into the marriage with certain expectations of the roles they would play. Joe would support them; JoJo would keep the home fires burning. That arrangement had worked for the first nineteen years of their marriage, until Celeste was born, but now JoJo needed more from her husband. She needed his emotional support when her own well ran dry—and Joe caught himself occasionally miffed that his wife spent so

Some siblings of children with mental challenges are more apt to have social problems and poor self-image. However, in families that work together and support each other but encourage independence, everyone grows stronger through the process.

much energy on their daughter that there was little left for him.

Inch by emotional inch, the two began to grow distant. They used to bowl together on weekends—but now JoJo was too tired. Joe took resentful refuge on the couch, watching endless games of football or other seasonal sports. He loved his daughter, yes, of course. But he missed his wife. He missed their life.

But when Celeste's small arms hugged both her parents together, Joe and JoJo's eyes would meet—and they knew they'd have to find a way over the bumps in their

An intellectual disability—also called mental retardation, when a person's mental abilities are below what is average— is caused when the brain is injured or a problem prevents the brain from developing normally. These problems can happen before a baby's birth while he or she is still growing inside the mother, during the baby's birth, or after the baby is born. Here are some things that can cause intellectual disabilities:

- When the mother has certain infections or illnesses while she is pregnant.
- When the mother takes certain medicines, illegal drugs, or drinks alcohol while she is pregnant.
- When there's a problem with the baby's genes, which are in every cell and determine how the body will develop.
- When the baby doesn't get enough oxygen while he or she is being born.
- When the baby—or child—gets a serious infection after birth.
- When—at any time in life—a serious head injury hurts the brain permanently, so that it can no longer work the same.

marriage to keep a stable home for their beloved daughter. They did their best and stuck it out.

Celeste continued to bring joy to her parents' lives, but it was difficult sometimes for them to be patient with her slow development. At five years old, she still could not talk. Then one day, as mother and daughter were driving to the store, Celeste said, "Mommy" in a clear, tinkly voice.

JoJo had to pull to the side of the road to dry her tears.

Celeste was *integrated* into regular classes from the time she started kindergarten. An aide sat at her side the entire day, helping her learn at her own rate. She might not have been the fastest learner when it came to arithmetic and reading, but she was one of the kindest and most sensitive children in her class. When someone was sad, Celeste was always the first to notice and to offer a comforting hug.

When the time came for her second-grade class to elect a president—the one child who would pass out papers in class and deliver mail through the hallways—they chose Celeste. She had trouble navigating the halls alone to distribute mail, so she chose a different friend to help her with her special presidential tasks every day. And every day, Celeste learned a little bit more of the delivery routine.

JoJo watches her child with pride. Who knew how far Celeste could go in life? Yes, she had Down

About 2.3 percent of all people have mental retardation. This means that in group of 100 people, at least 2 are likely to have intellectual disabilities.

syndrome—but what did that really mean in terms of limitations?

When the class gathered in front of the TV to watch the first-ever inauguration of an African-American president, Celeste watched Barack Obama with a big grin.

"Now he's the president," she said, turning to her mom with shining eyes. "Just like me!"

HEADLINES

(Adapted from "Siblings of Children with Mental Retardation: Family Characteristics and Adjustment," *Journal of Child and Family Studies,* April 01, 2005)

Researchers have found that the siblings of children with mental retardation may be at greater risk for adjustment problems because of family stress. Clearly, dealing with a child with mental retardation is stressful for all family members. Research also shows, however, that families can overcome this stress.

What did the researchers find? Children with siblings who have mental retardation are more apt to have a poor self-concept; they had more social problems. This was particularly true for families where parents were unable to cope with their own stress. But this was *not* true for siblings of children with mental retardation when they were part of families who stick together and who encouraged independence in their children.

What Do You Think?

Why do you think the brothers or sisters of children with mental retardation are more apt to have problems both socially and with their self-concept? What did the researchers find made a difference in families like these? Does this make sense to you? Why or why not?

HEADLINES

(From "Down's Syndrome and Sibling Love" by Glenn Collins, *New York Times*, April 19, 2009)

"Well, I wiggle her all around, see," said 7-year-old Sean Cohan, as he attempted to describe, as precisely as possible, exactly what it was like to have a 3 1/2-year-old sister who has Down's syndrome. "Then she wiggles me all around," he said, "and she jumps on me. Then she jumps on my dad. And that makes me laugh a little, and it makes my dad laugh a lot!"

Had he forgotten to describe anything? "Well, sometimes she beats the heck out of me," he said, giggling

as his sister Alexis came over and gave him a huge hug.

The sentiments, however, were not all giddy. "Really, it's not Down's syndrome I worry about," said 13-year-old Judy Garczynski about her 6-month-old sister, Megan. "But my sister has a heart condition, and she might not make it." She paused a moment, amid the silence of the other children around her. "We take it one day at a time."

It was Sibling Day at the school of the Association for Children With Down's Syndrome in Bellmore, L.I., and 39 children from 21 families had come to visit their brothers' and sisters' school on a recent morning.

Sometimes movingly, sometimes hilariously, they shared their experiences with other children whose siblings have Down's syndrome. They talked about the cruel teasing of friends and the ignorance of neighbors and even teachers. . . .

One of the problems that older siblings have is coping with the word "retard," which is commonly used as a *pejorative* among children. "With the other kids, you have to explain to them—that they're talking about your brother," said 12-year-old Todd Probeck of Wantaugh, L.I., whose 3-year-old brother, Danny, has Down's syndrome. "I don't think lots of kids really know what they're saying."

What Do You Think?

Why do you think kids make fun of people with disabilities? How does the author of this article explain this sort of cruelty? Do you think he is right? Why or why not?

Find Out More
BOOKS

Baskin, Amy and Heather Fawcett. *More Than a Mom: Living a Full and Balanced Life When Your Child has Special Needs.* Bethesda, Md.: Woodbine House, 2006.

Brodey, Denise. *The Elephant in the Playroom: Ordinary Parents Write Intimately and Honestly About the Extraordinary Highs and Heartbreaking Lows of Raising Kids with Special Needs.* New York: Hudson Street Press, 2007.

Dowling, Cindy, Neil Nicoll, and Bernadette Thomas. *A Different Kind of Perfect: Writings by Parents on Raising a Child with Special Needs.* Boston: Trumpeter Books, 2004.

Hooper, Stephen R. and Warren Umansky. *Young Children with Special Needs.* 5th ed. Upper Saddle River, N.J.: Prentice Hall, 2008.

McIntosh, Kenneth and Phyllis Livingston. *Youth with Juvenile Schizophrenia: The Search for Reality.* Broomall, Penn.: Mason Crest Publishers, 2007.

Meyer, Don, ed. *The Sibling Slam Book: What it's Really Like to Have a Brother or Sister with Special Needs.* Bethesda, Md.: Woodbine Press, 2005.

Siegel, Bryna and Stuart Silverstein. *What About Me? Growing Up with a Developmentally Disabled Sibling.* Cambridge, Mass.: Perseus Publishing, 2001.

Sirof, Harriet. *The Road Back: Living with a Physical Disability.* Lincoln, Neb.: iUniverse.com, 2000.

Whiteman, Nancy J. and Linda Roan-Yager. *Building a Joyful Life with Your Child Who Has Special Needs.* Philadelphia: Jessica Kingsley Publishers, 2007.

Winter, Judy. *Breakthrough Parenting for Children with Special Needs: Raising the Bar of Expectations.* San Francisco: Jossey-Bass, 2006.

ON THE INTERNET

Beach Center on Disability
www.beachcenter.org

Children's Disabilities
Information
www.childrensdisabilities.info

Comeunity: Children's Disabilities and Special Needs
www.comeunity.com

Families Together for People
with Disabilities
www.familiestogether.org

Family Village: A Global
Community of Disability-
Related Resources
www.familyvillage.wisc.edu

Kids Together, Inc.
www.kidstogether.org

National Dissemination Center
for Children with Disabilities
www.nichcy.org

Special Child: For Parents of
Children with Disabilities
www.specialchild.com

Support for Families of Children with Disabilities
www.supportforfamilies.org

Through the Looking Glass
Web Site
lookingglass.org

Bibliography

CNN Interactive. www.cnn.com/HEALTH/9810/15/schizo.reality

Collins, Glenn. "Down's Syndrome and Sibling Love." *New York Times*, April 19, 2009.

Journal of Child and Family Studies. "Siblings of Children with Mental Retardation: Family Characteristics and Adjustment," April 01, 2005.

Klein, Stan & Schive, Kim. *You Will Dream New Dreams: Inspiring Personal Stories by Parents of Children with Disabilities*. New York: Kensington Books, 2000.

Lavin, Judith. *Special Kids Need Special Parents*. New York: Berkley Books, 2001.

Naseef, Robert. *Special Children, Challenged Parents*. Baltimore: Paul H. Brookes, 2001.

National Institute of Mental Health. www.nimh.nih.gov/health/publications/schizophrenia.

Marriage and Family Encyclopedia. family.jrank.org/pages/399/Disabilities.html.

Marsh, Diane T. *Troubled Journey: Coming to Terms with the Mental Illness of a Sibling or Parent*. New York: Tarcher, 1997.

Rowley, Judy. "Welcoming Babies with Spina Bifida." June 2007. www.waisman.wisc.edu/~Rowley/sb-kids/wbwsb.html

Schizophrenia.com. www.schizophrenia.com/family/FAQsibs.htm# sibeffe

ndex

About the Author and the Consultant

AUTHOR

Julianna Fields is the pseudonym of a Gannett human interest columnist whose byline has also appeared in *Writer's Digest*, *American History*, *American Woodworker* and hundreds of other publications, as well as educational workbooks and a guidebook about Steamtown, a National Park Service site in Scranton, Pennsylvania. She's also a writing coach and editor.

CONSULTANT

Gallup has studied human nature and behavior for more than seventy years. Gallup's reputation for delivering relevant, timely, and visionary research on what people around the world think and feel is the cornerstone of the organization. Gallup employs many of the world's leading scientists in management, economics, psychology, and sociology, and its consultants assist leaders in identifying and monitoring behavioral economic indicators worldwide. Gallup consultants help organizations boost organic growth by increasing customer engagement and maximizing employee productivity through measurement tools, coursework, and strategic advisory services. Gallup's 2,000 professionals deliver services at client organizations, through the Web, at Gallup University's campuses, and in forty offices around the world.